This Book Belongs to:

```
_____
_____
```

Test Your Colors Here

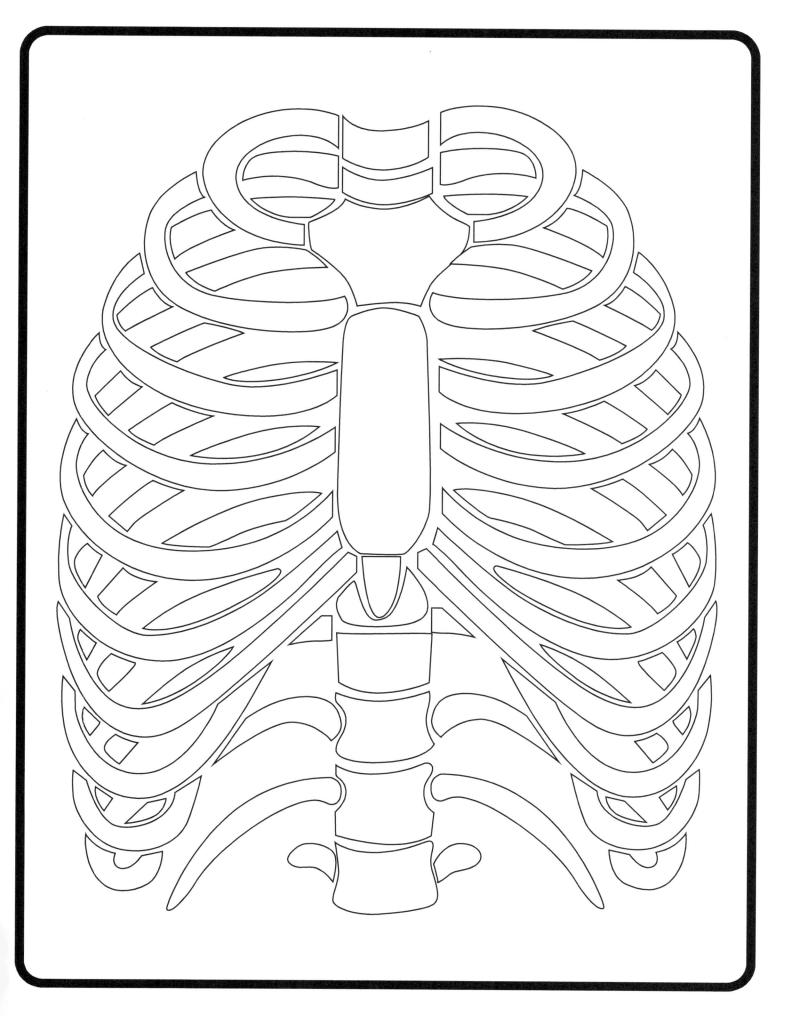

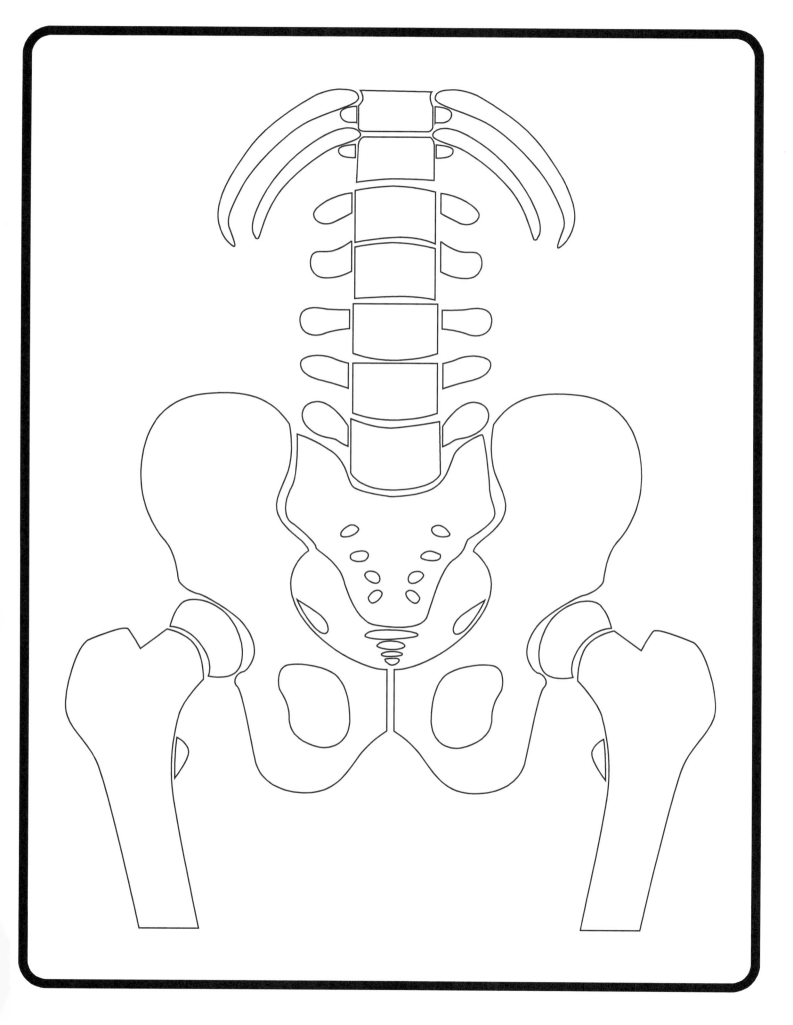

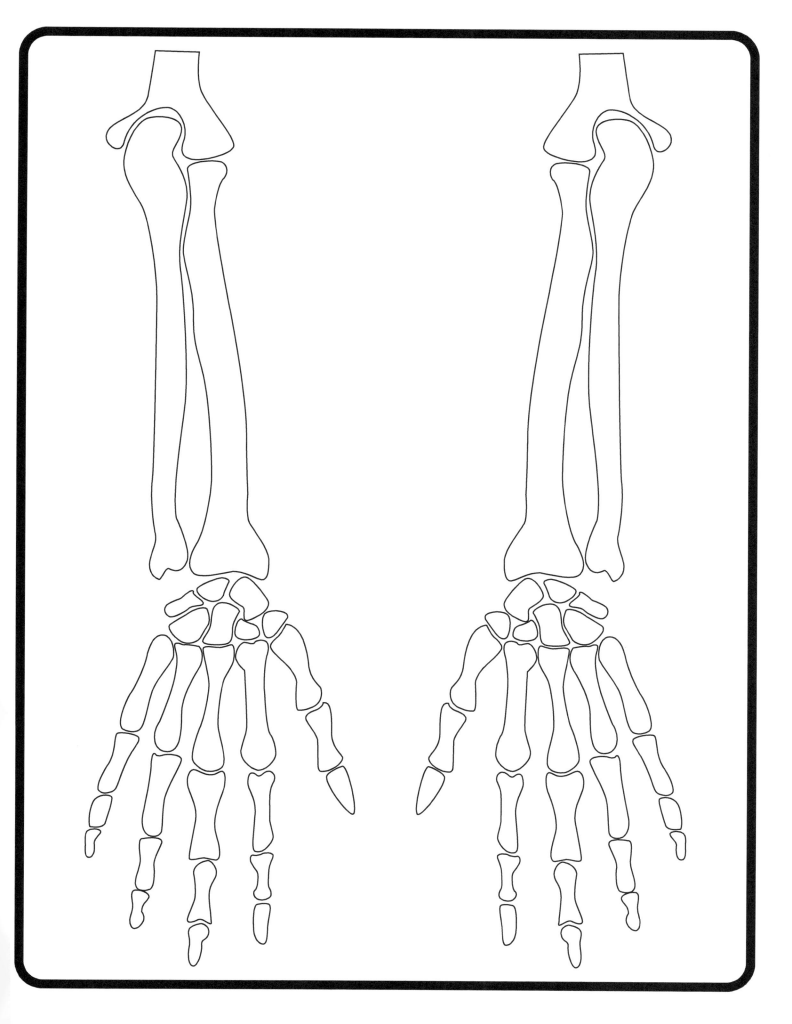

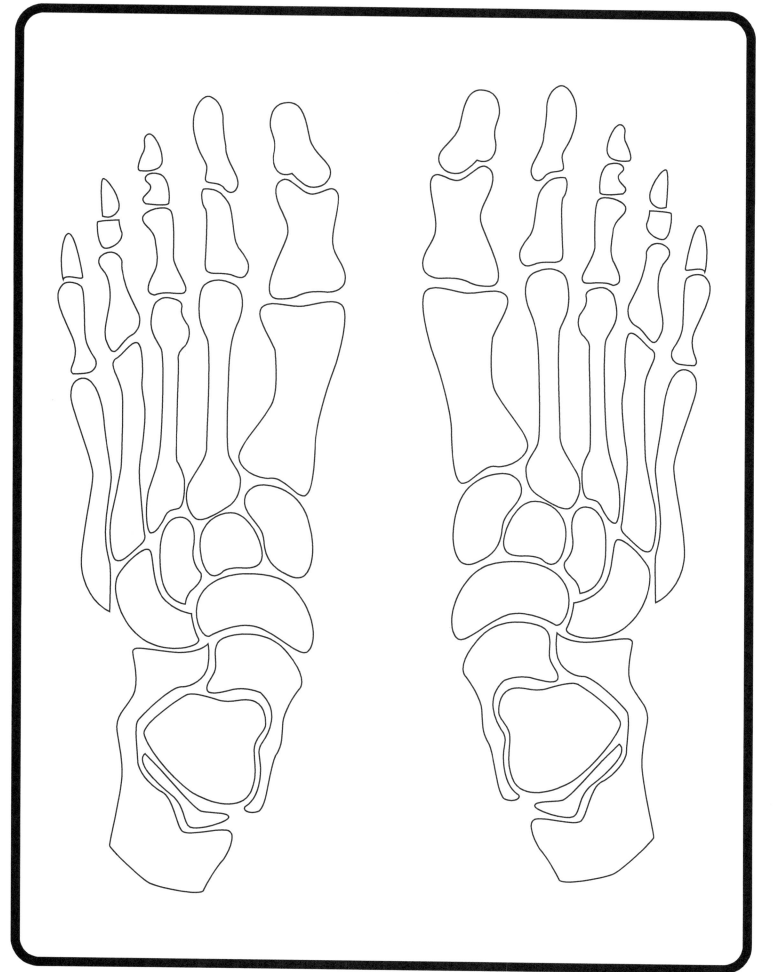

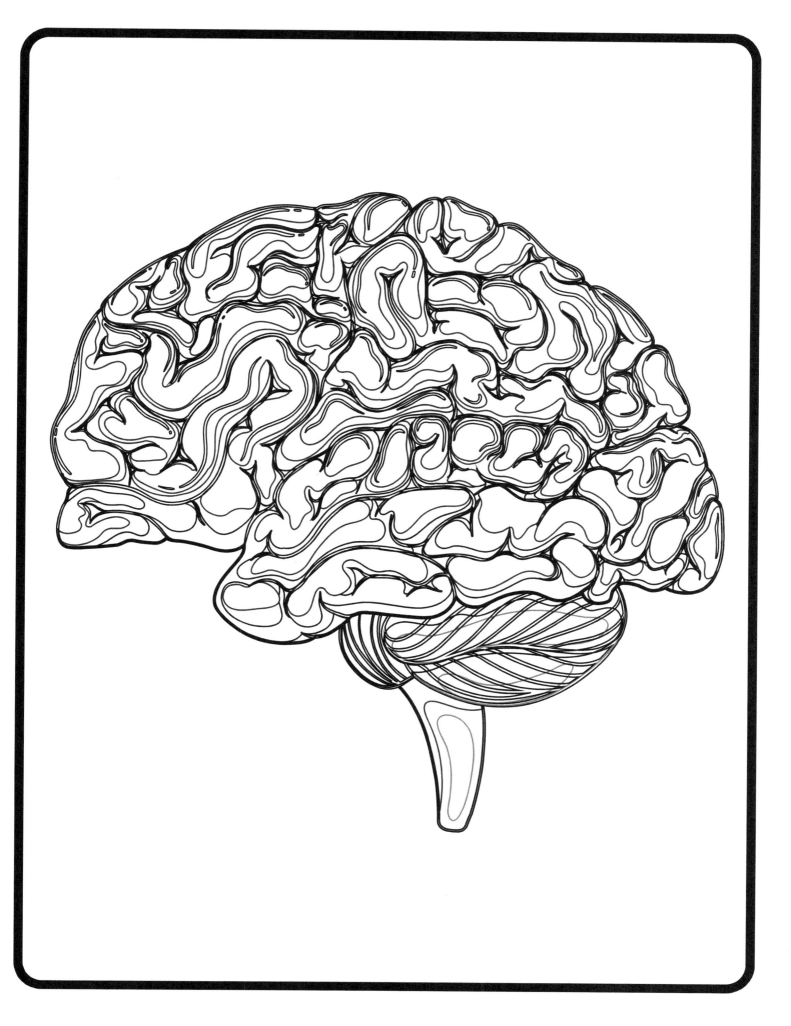

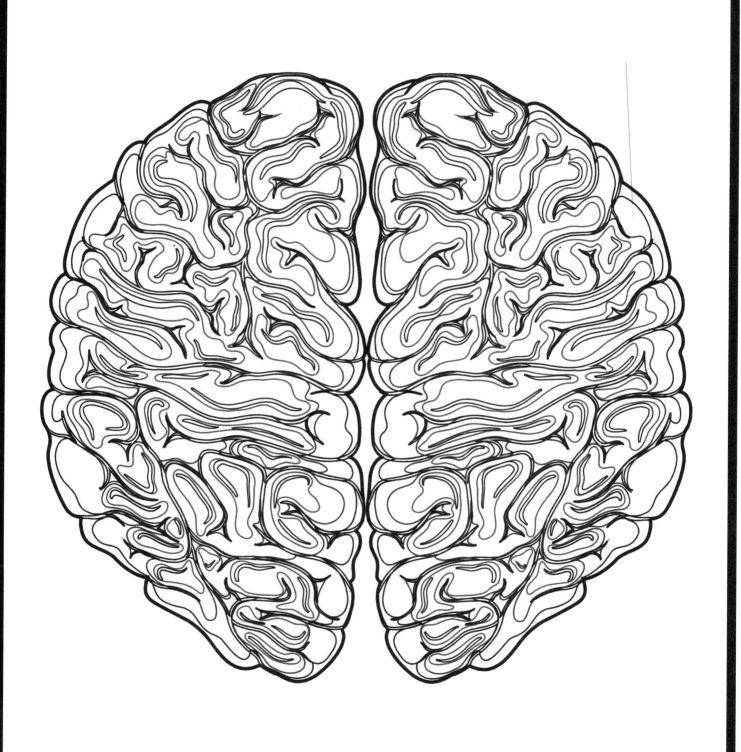

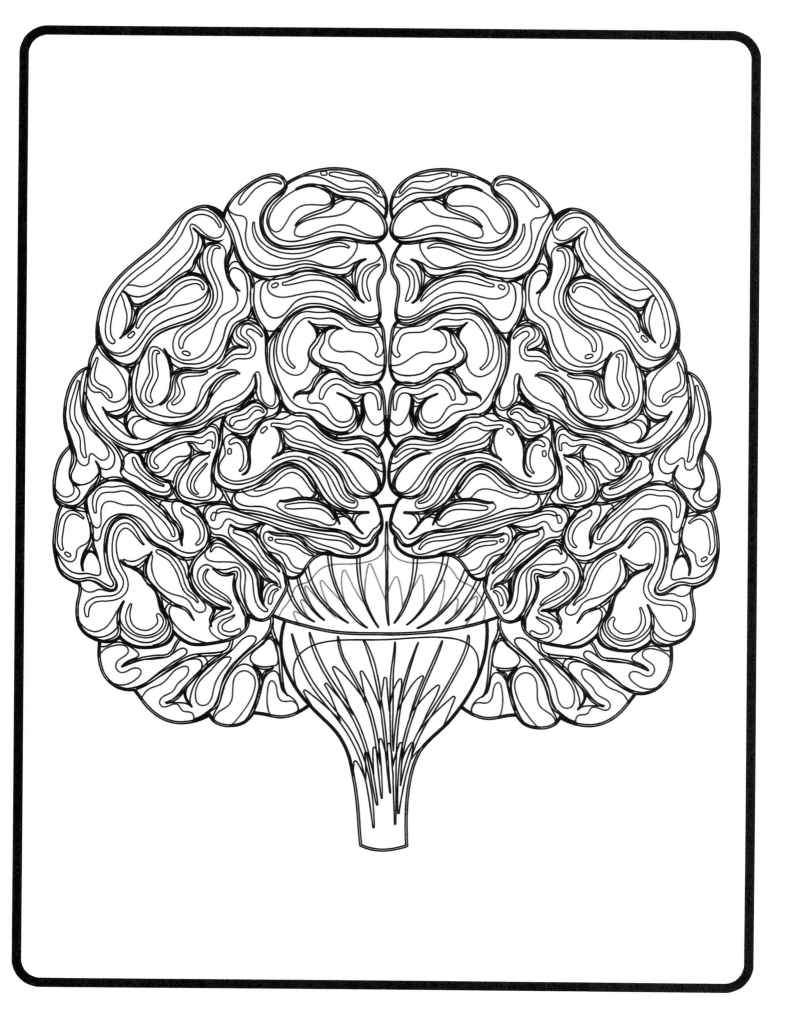

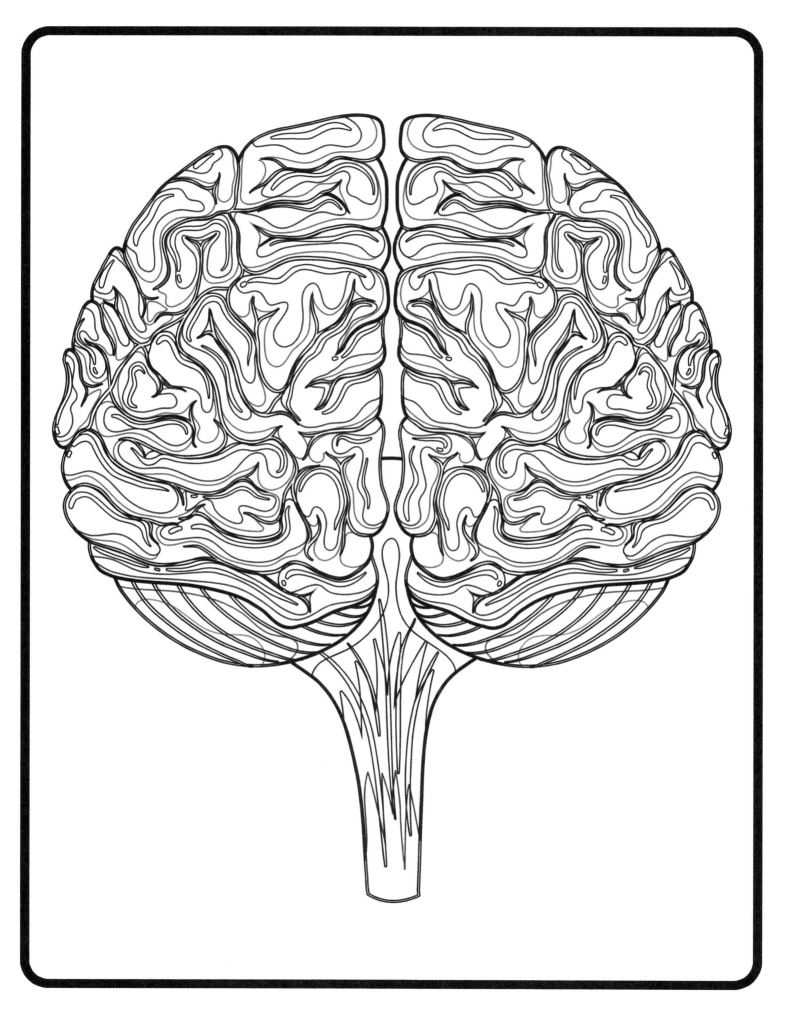

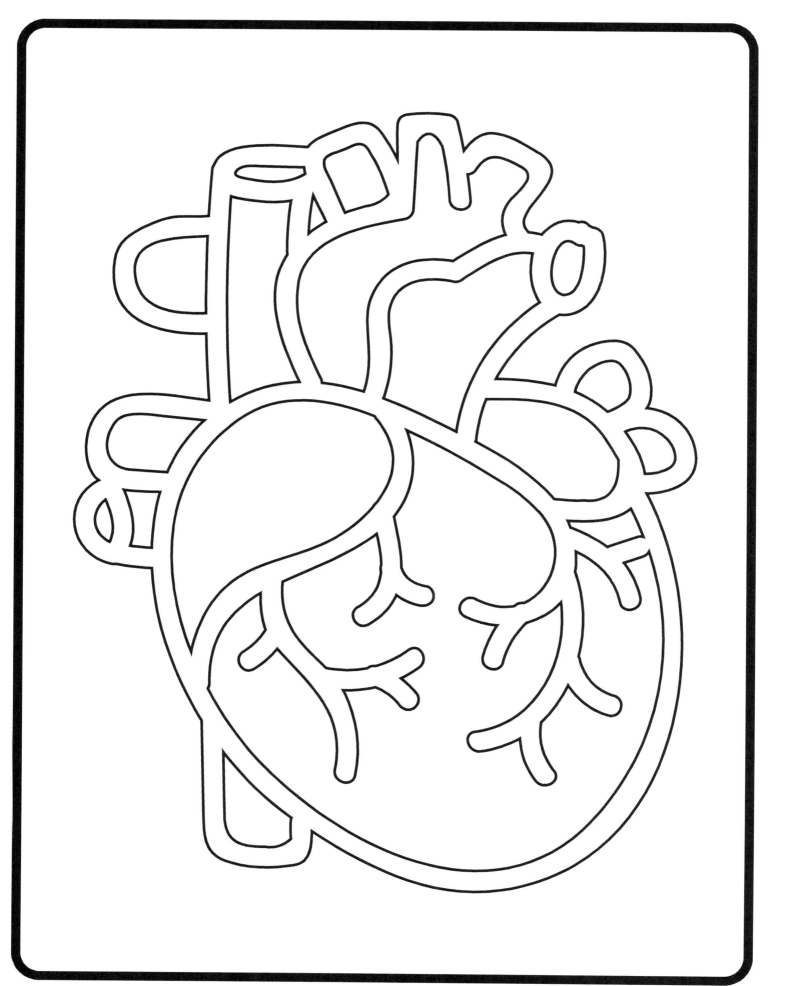

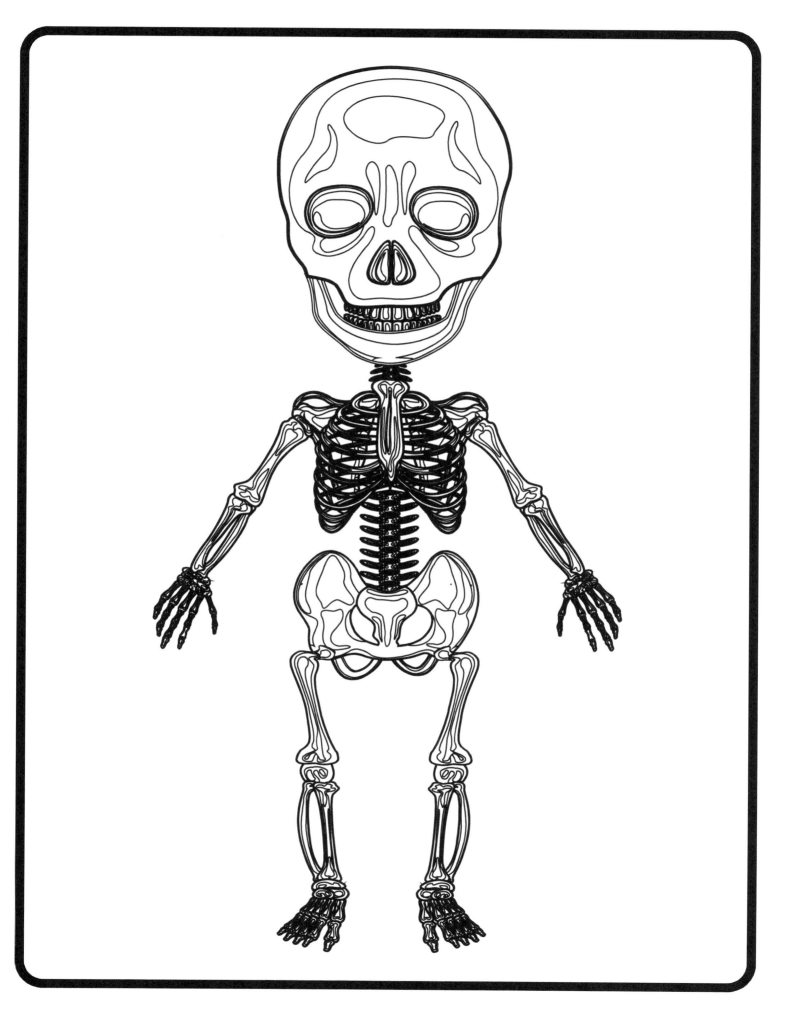

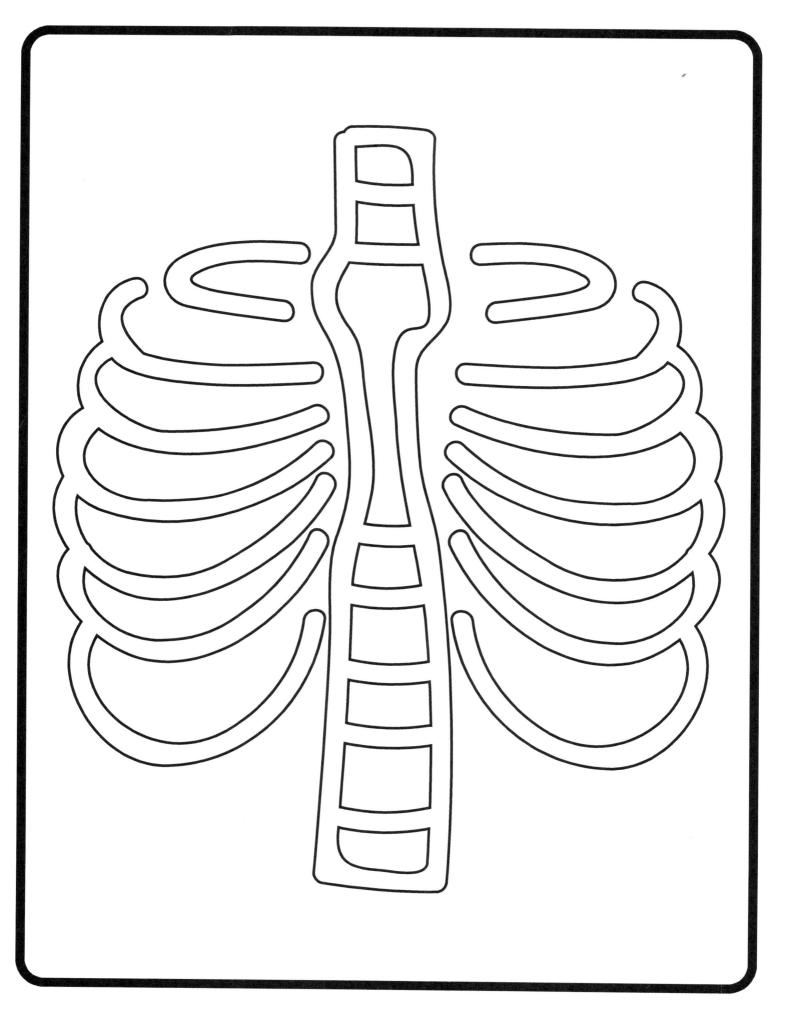

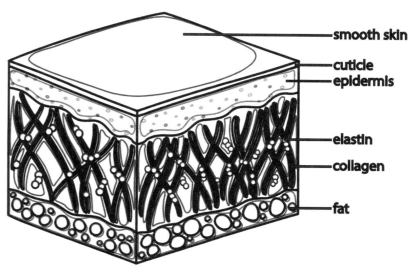

Aged Skin Section

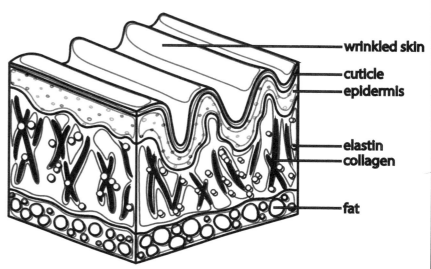

Gout (Inflamatory Arthritis)

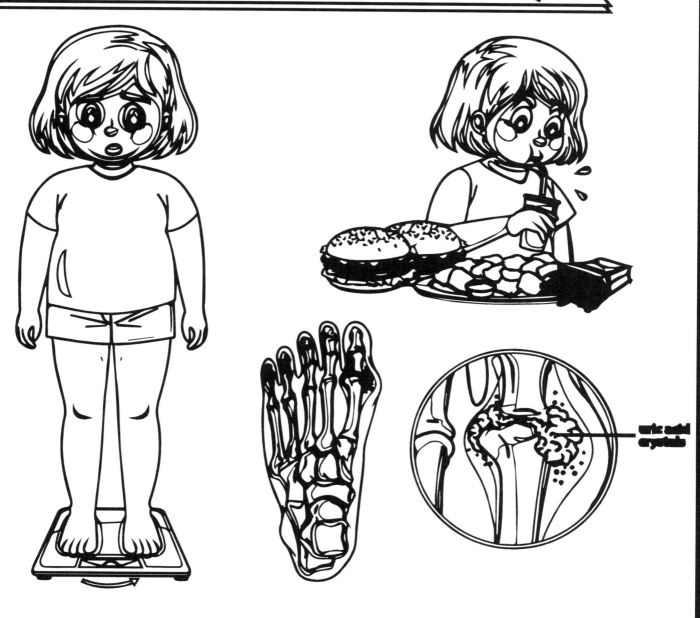

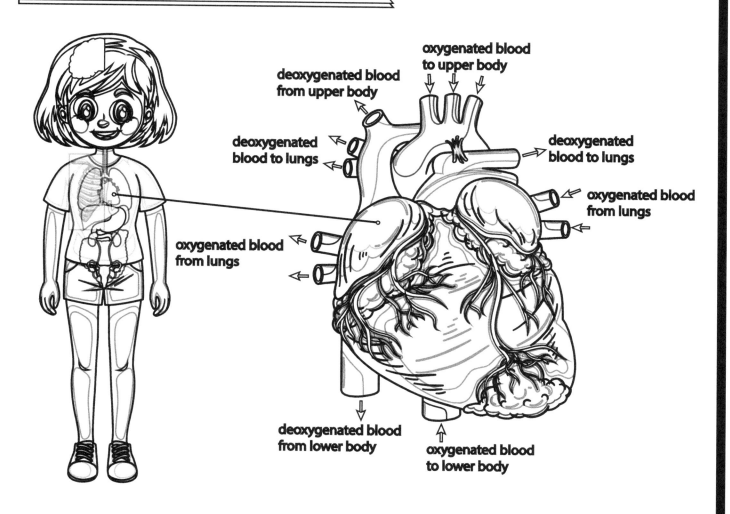

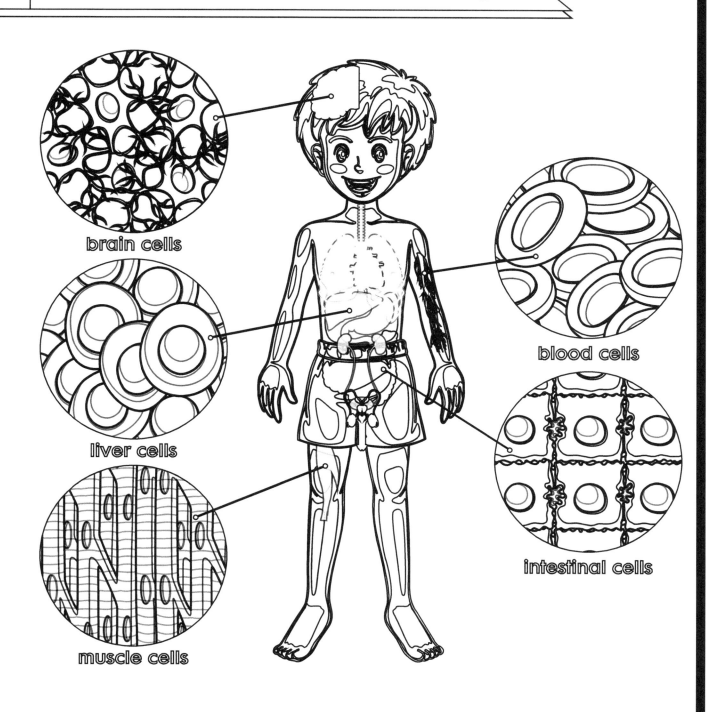

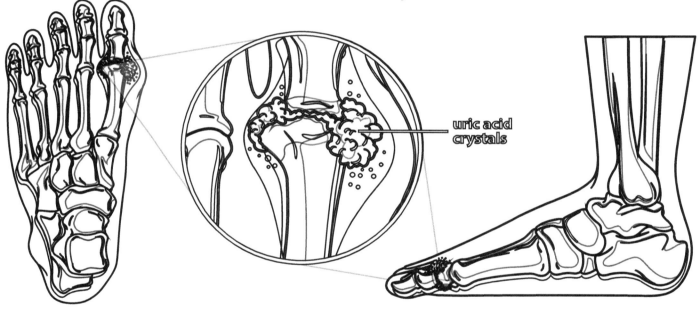

Gout (Inflamatory Arthritis)

uric acid crystals

Gout (Inflamatory Arthritis)

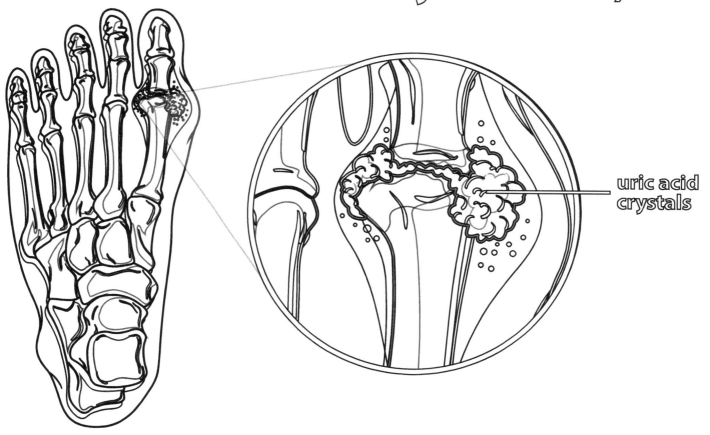

Strangulated Hernia

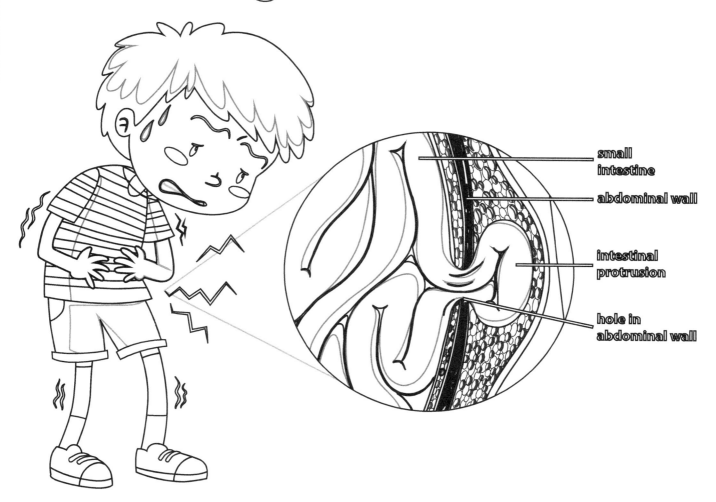

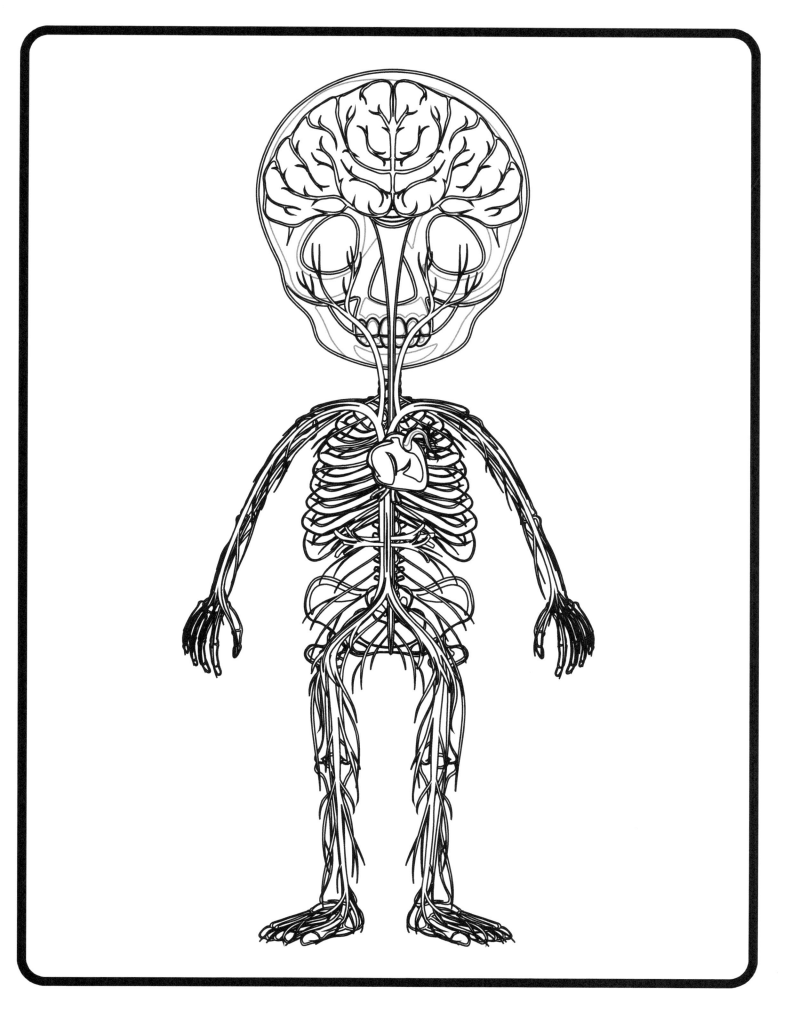

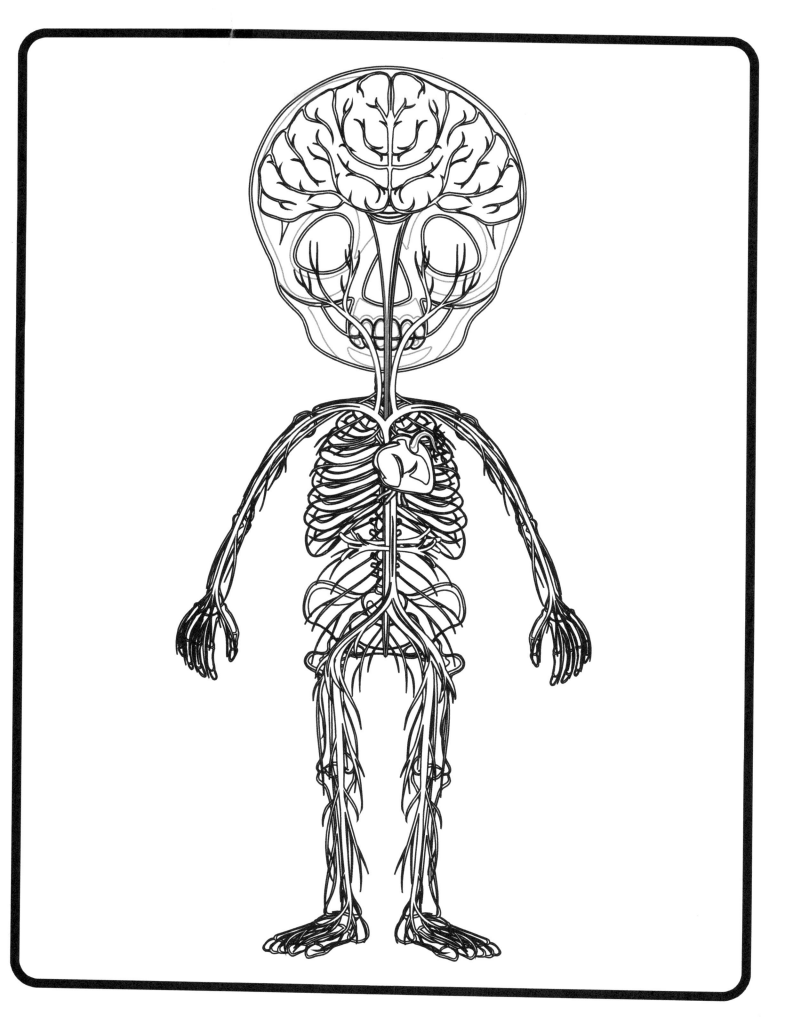

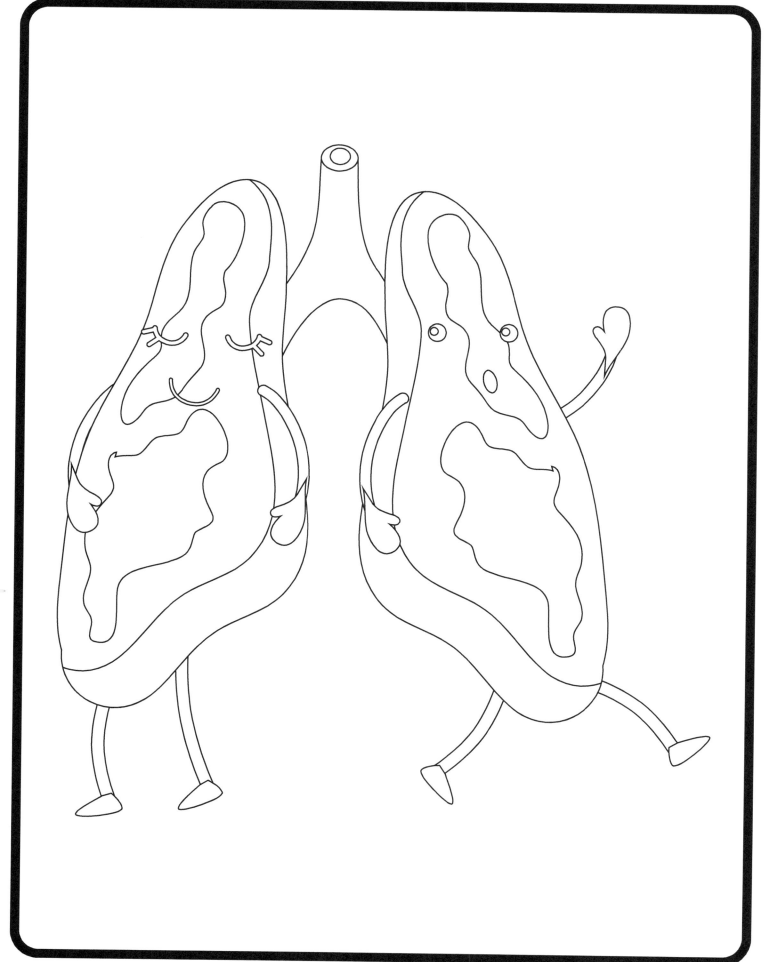

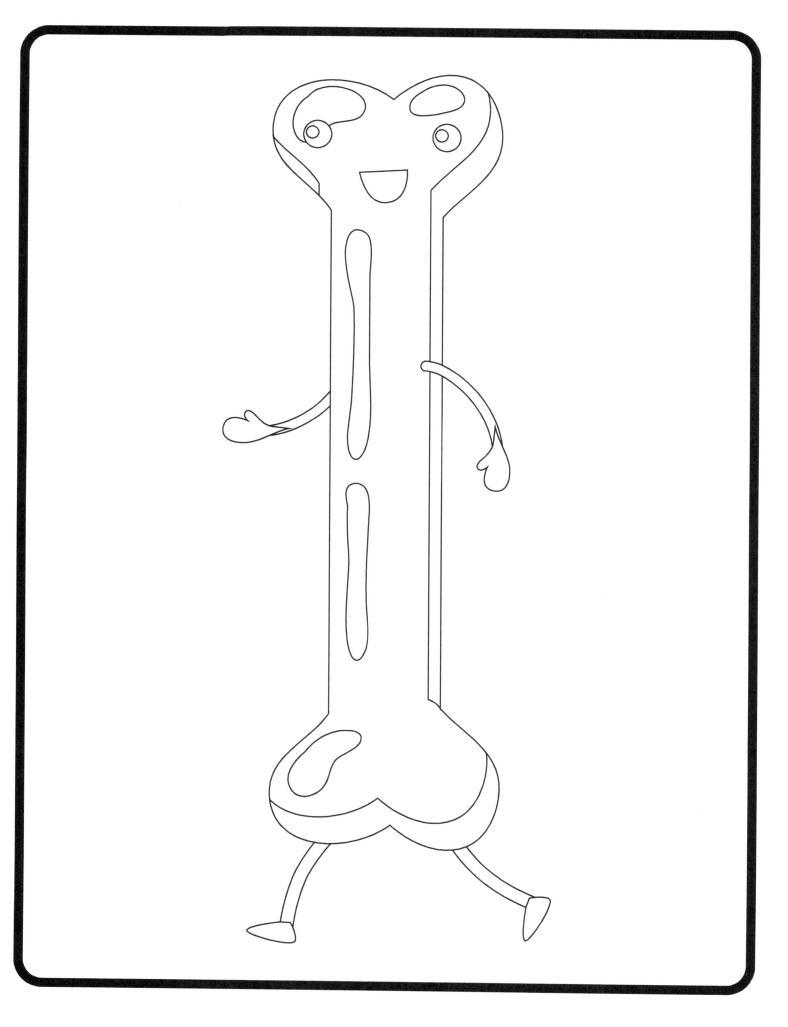

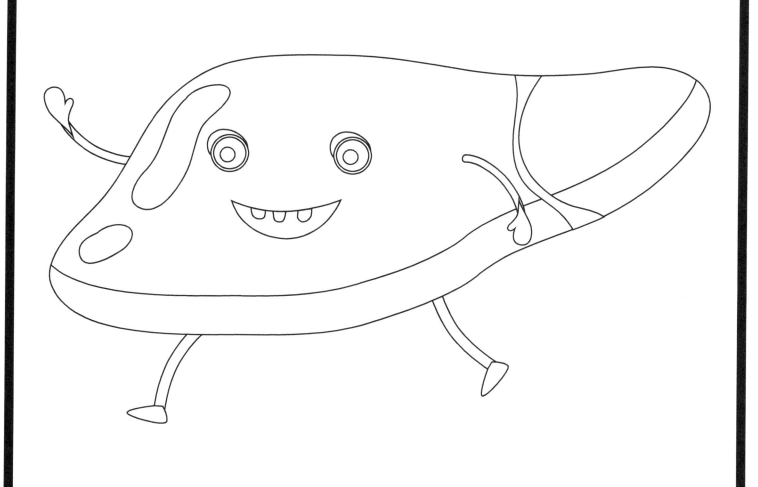